HAL•LEONARD
ESSENTIAL SONGS

PIANO VOCAL GUITAR

The 1980s

ISBN 0-634-09101-8

HAL•LEONARD®
CORPORATION
7777 W. BLUEMOUND RD. P.O. BOX 13819 MILWAUKEE, WI 53213

Visit Hal Leonard Online at
www.halleonard.com

CONTENTS

200	I Just Called to Say I Love You	Stevie Wonder	1	1984
205	I Love a Rainy Night	Eddie Rabbitt	1	1981
210	It's My Life	Talk Talk	31	1984
216	Jessie's Girl	Rick Springfield	1	1981
222	Jump	Van Halen	1	1984
230	Kiss on My List	Daryl Hall & John Oates	1	1981
236	Lady	The Whispers	28	1980
250	Lady in Red	Chris DeBurgh	3	1987
254	Legs	ZZ Top	8	1984
260	Man in the Mirror	Michael Jackson	1	1988
270	Manic Monday	Bangles	2	1986
274	Material Girl	Madonna	2	1985
243	Missing You	John Waite	1	1984
278	Nasty	Janet Jackson	3	1986
285	Nothing's Gonna Stop Us Now	Starship	1	1987
290	Oh Sherrie	Steve Perry	3	1984
298	On the Wings of Love	Jeffrey Osborne	29	1982
304	The Search Is Over	Survivor	4	1985
308	Seven Bridges Road	Eagles	21	1981
314	Should I Stay or Should I Go	The Clash	50	1983
318	Sister Christian	Night Ranger	5	1984
321	Somewhere Out There	Linda Ronstadt & James Ingram	2	1987
326	Steppin' Out	Joe Jackson	6	1982
334	Straight Up	Paula Abdul	1	1989
338	Stray Cat Strut	Stray Cats	3	1983
342	Take My Breath Away (Love Theme)	Berlin	1	1986
352	Tempted	Squeeze	49	1981
356	Time After Time	Cyndi Lauper	1	1984
360	Up Where We Belong	Joe Cocker & Jennifer Warnes	1	1982
364	Video Killed the Radio Star	The Buggles	40	1980
370	Wanted Dead or Alive	Bon Jovi	7	1987
376	The Warrior	Scandal	7	1984
382	We Are the World	USA For Africa	1	1985
388	What About Love?	Heart	10	1985
347	What's Love Got to Do with It	Tina Turner	1	1984
392	White Wedding	Billy Idol	36	1983

ABRACADABRA

Words and Music by
STEVE MILLER

D.S. al Coda

AGAINST ALL ODDS
(Take a Look at Me Now)

Words and Music by
PHIL COLLINS

Moderately slow

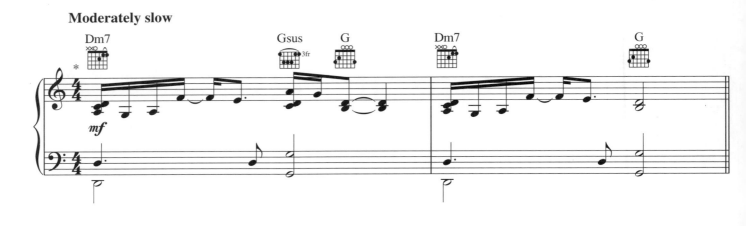

How can I just let you walk a-way, just let you leave with-out __ a trace, when I

stand here tak-ing ev-'ry breath __ with you? __ Ooh. _____ You're the

* Recorded a half step lower.

AGAINST THE WIND

Words and Music by
BOB SEGER

noth - in' left ___ to burn ___ and noth - in' left to prove. ___
wor - ried a - bout pay - in', or e - ven how much I owed. ___

End instrumental

And I re - mem - ber what she ___ said to
Mov - in' eight miles a min - ute for months at a
Well, those drift - er's days are ___ past me

me, ___ how she swore ___ that it nev - er would end. ___
time, ___ break - in' all ___ of the rules ___ that would bend, ___
now. ___ I've got so ___ much more to ___ think a - bout: ___

I re-mem-ber how she held __ me oh so tight, ____
I be-gan to find __ my-self search - in',
dead - lines __ and com - mit - ments,

Wish I did - n't know now what I did - n't know then.
search-in' for shel - ter a - gain and a - gain.
what to leave in, what to leave out.

A - gainst the wind, __
A - gainst the wind, __
A - gainst the wind, __

we were run - nin' a - gainst __ the wind. __
lit - tle some-thin' a - gainst __ the wind. __
I'm still run - nin' a - gainst __ the wind. __

We were
I
I'm

To Coda

young and strong. __ We were run-nin' a-gainst __ the wind.
found my-self __ seek-in' shel-ter a-gainst __ the wind.
old-er now, __ but still run-nin' a-gainst __ the wind.

D.S. al Coda

CODA

Well, I'm old - er now, __ and still run-nin' a-gainst the

Repeat and Fade

wind, a-gainst the wind. A-gainst the

ALL NIGHT LONG
(All Night)

Words and Music by
LIONEL RICHIE

CALL ME
from the Paramount Motion Picture AMERICAN GIGOLO

Words by DEBORAH HARRY
Music by GIORGIO MORODER

ALMOST PARADISE

Love Theme from the Paramount Motion Picture FOOTLOOSE

Words by DEAN PITCHFORD
Music by ERIC CARMEN

AMANDA

Words and Music by TOM SCHOLZ

AXEL F
Theme from the Paramount Motion Picture BEVERLY HILLS COP

By HAROLD FALTERMEYER

Moderately fast, with a strong beat

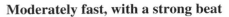

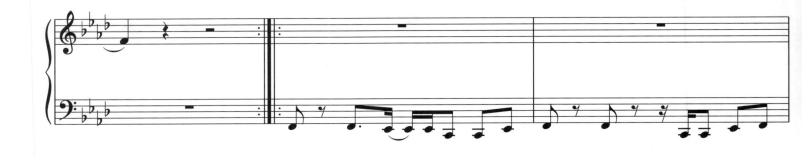

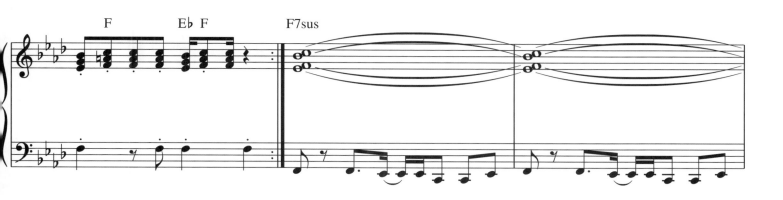

BABY, COME TO ME

Words and Music by
ROD TEMPERTON

Moderately

Thlnk-in' back in time, __ when love was on-ly in the mind, __ I re-al-ize
Spend-in' ev-'ry dime __ to keep you talk-in' on the line, __ that's how it was,

ain't no sec-ond chance; __ you've got to hold on to ro-mance. __ Don't
and all those walks to-geth - er out in an - y kind of weath - er, just be-

CARRIE

Words and Music by
JOEY TEMPEST and MIC MICHAELI

CHARIOTS OF FIRE

from CHARIOTS OF FIRE

Music by VANGELIS

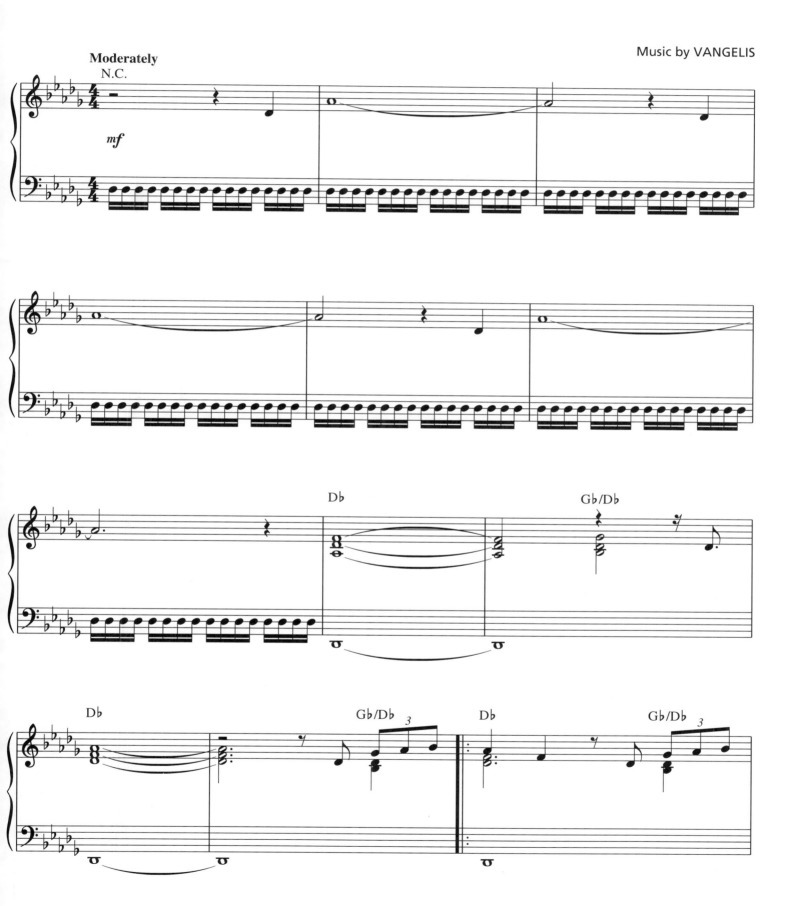

CENTERFOLD

Written by SETH JUSTMAN

CRAZY LITTLE THING CALLED LOVE

Words and Music by
FREDDIE MERCURY

mo - tor bike __ un - til I'm read - y.　　Cra - zy lit - tle thing called

love.

I got - ta be cool, ____ re - lax, ____ a - get hip, ____ a - get on my tracks. Take a back seat, ____ hitch - hike ____ to take a lit - tle long ____ ride ____ on my

DANGER ZONE
from the Motion Picture TOP GUN

Words and Music by GIORGIO MORODER
and TOM WHITLOCK

Rev - in' up your en - gine; lis - ten to her howl - in' roar. _____
Head - in' in the twi - light spread - in' out her wings _ to - night. _____
Out a - long the edge is al - ways where I burn _ to be. _____

High - way to the dan - ger zone; ___

right in - to the dan - ger zone. ___

Repeat and Fade

DIDN'T WE ALMOST HAVE IT ALL

Words and Music by WILL JENNINGS
and MICHAEL MASSER

Slowly

Re-mem-ber when we held on in the rain, the nights we al-most
The way you used to touch me felt so fine; we kept our hearts to-

lost it; once a-gain we can take the night in-to to-
geth-er; down the line, a mo-ment in the soul can last for-

DON'T DO ME LIKE THAT

Words and Music by
TOM PETTY

(1.) I was talk-in' with a friend of mine, said a wom-an had hurt his pride. __
(2., D.S.) Lis-ten, hon-ey, can you see? Ba-by, it would bur-y me ___

DOIN' IT
(All for My Baby)

Words and Music by PHIL CODY
and MIKE DUKE

Early in the mornin' ___ I'm still in bed. ___
Lat-er in the eve-nin' it's been a bus-y day.

She comes to me with sweet af-fec - tion. _____
She lays her head up-on my wea-ry shoul - der. _____

93

DON'T YOU
(Forget About Me)
from the Universal Picture THE BREAKFAST CLUB

Words and Music by KEITH FORSEY
and STEVE SCHIFF

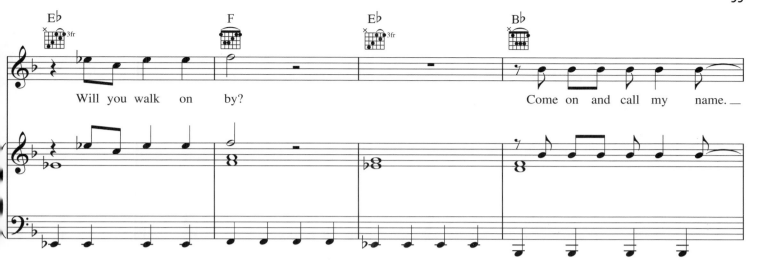

Will you walk on by?   Come on and call my name.

Will you call my name?   I say ooh

Repeat and Fade

la,   la, la, la,_____   la, la, la, la,_____   la, la, la,   la, la,   la, la, la, la.

DREAMER

Words and Music by RICK DAVIES
and ROGER HODGSON

you can do some - thing.) If I could do an - y - thing... (But can you do some - thing

out _____ of this world?) _____

Bb/C

C

Take a dream on a Sun - day.

Gm7/C

cresc. little by little

EBONY AND IVORY

Words and Music by
PAUL McCARTNEY

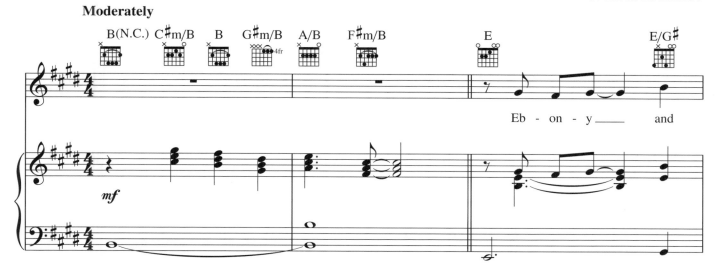

Moderately

Eb-on-y ___ and

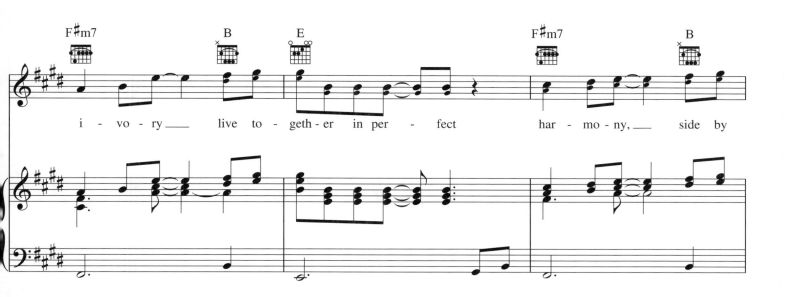

i-vo-ry ___ live to-geth-er in per-fect har-mo-ny, ___ side by

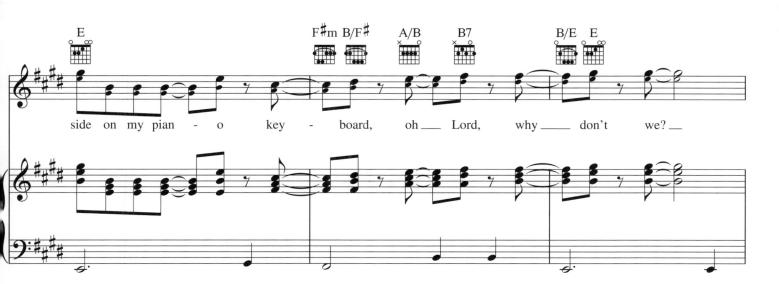

side on my pian-o key-board, oh ___ Lord, why ___ don't we? ___

EVEN THE NIGHTS ARE BETTER

Words and Music by J. L. WALLACE,
TERRY SKINNER and KEN BELL

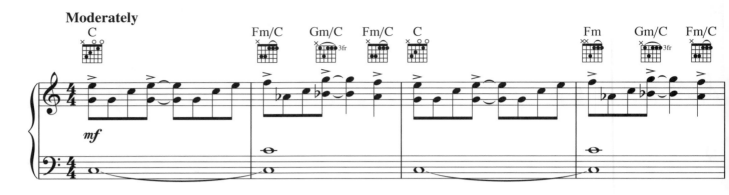

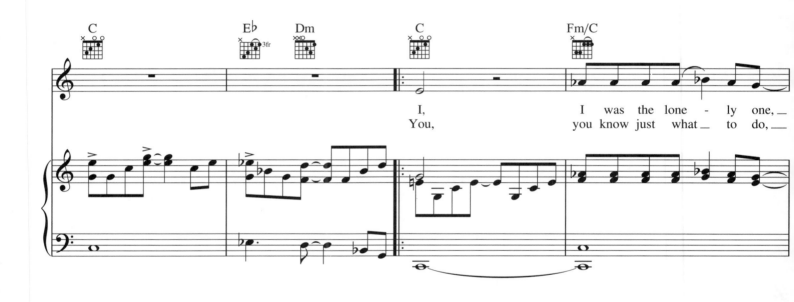

EVERYBODY WANTS TO RULE THE WORLD

Words and Music by IAN STANLEY,
ROLAND ORZABAL and CHRIS HUGHES

wants to rule the world.

world. There's a room where the light won't find you

hold - ing hands while the walls come tum - bling down. When they do, I'll be

right be - hind you. So glad we've al - most made it. So sad they

Additional Lyrics

Verse 2:

It's my own design,
It's my own remorse,
Help me to decide.
Help me make the most
Of freedom and of pleasure,
Nothing ever lasts forever.
Everybody wants to rule the world.

Chorus 2:

I can't stand this indecision
Married with a lack of vision.
Everybody wants to rule the world.

Chorus 3:

Say that you'll never, never, never, need it.
One headline, why believe it?
Everybody wants to rule the world.

Chorus 4:

All for freedom and for pleasure,
Nothing ever lasts forever.
Everybody wants to rule the world.

FOREVER YOUNG

Words and Music by ROD STEWART, JIM CREGAN,
KEVIN SAVIGAR and BOB DYLAN

round you when you're far___ from home. ___ And may you

grow ___ to be proud, ___ dig - ni - fied ___ and true. ___
for - tune be with you, may your guid - ing light ___ be strong, ___
fi - n'lly fly a - way, I'll be hop - ing that I served ___ you well. ___

___ And do un - to oth - ers as
___ build a stair-way to heav - en with a
___ For all the wis-dom of a life - time,

you'd have done to you. _____
prince or a vag - a - bond. _____
no one can ev - er tell. _____

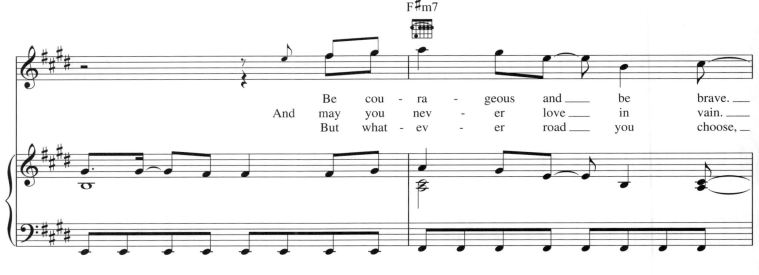

Be cou - ra - geous and _____ be brave. _____
And may you nev - er love _____ in vain. _____
But what - ev - er road _____ you choose, _____

_____ And in my heart you'll al - ways stay _____
_____ And in my heart you will _____ re - main _____
_____ I'm right be - hind you win _____ or lose, _

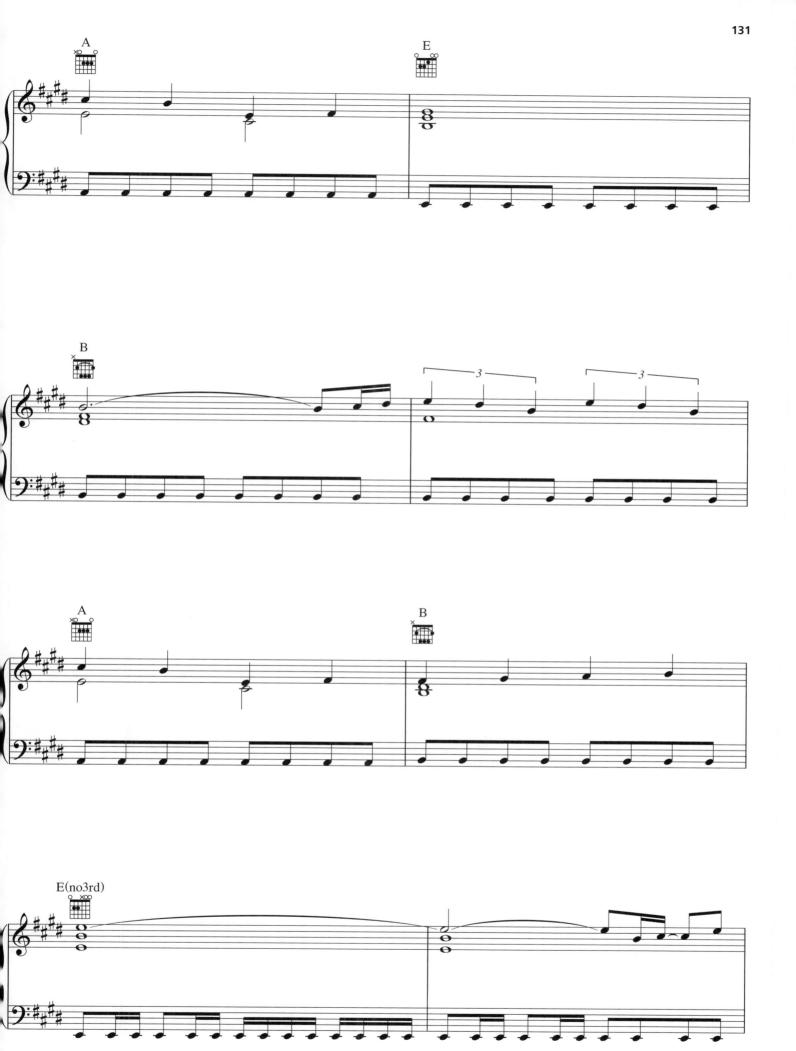

GIVE ME THE NIGHT

Words and Music by
ROD TEMPERTON

Moderately Fast, with funky feeling

Verse 2. You need the evenin' action, a place to dine.
A glass of wine, a little late romance.
It's a chain reaction.
We'll see the people of the world comin' out to dance.
'Cause there's. . . Chorus

Verse 3. (Instrumental)
'Cause there's. . . Chorus

Verse 4. And if we stay together,
We'll feel the rhythm of evening takin' us up high.
Never mind the weather.
We'll be dancin' in the street until the morning light.
'Cause there's. . . Chorus

GLORIA

Original Words and Music by GIANCARLO BIGAZZI
and UMBERTO TOZZI
English Lyrics by TREVOR VEITCH

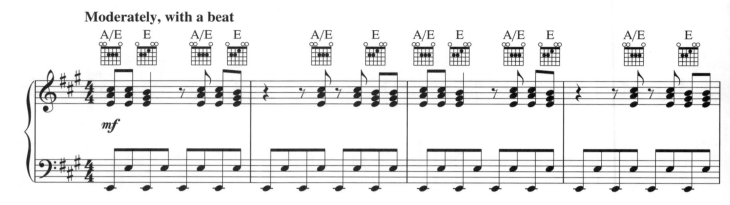

Moderately, with a beat

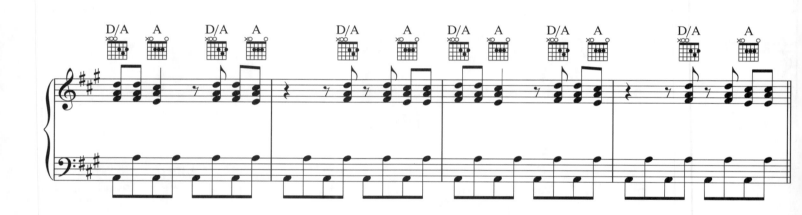

Glo-ri-a,   you're al-ways on the run now.   Run-nin' af-ter some-
Glo-ri-a,   how's it gon-na go down?   Will you meet him on the

HARD HABIT TO BREAK

Words and Music by STEPHEN KIPNER
and JOHN LEWIS PARKER

HEARTBREAKER

Words and Music by CLIFF WADE
and GEOFF GILL

You're the right __ kind of sin-

-ner to re-lease __ my in-ner fan-ta-sy, __

THE HEAT IS ON
from the Paramount Motion Picture BEVERLY HILLS COP

Words by KEITH FORSEY
Music by HAROLD FALTERMEYER

The heat is on, __ on __ the street. __ The heat is

on. The heat is on.

The heat is... on!

Vocal 1st time only

1 - 3

HERE I GO AGAIN

Words and Music by
BERNIE MARSDEN and DAVID COVERDALE

I don't know where I'm go - ing,
Though I keep searching for an ans - wer,

but I sure know where I've been.___
I never seem to find what I'm looking for.___

Hang-ing on the pro-mi-ses___ in___
Oh Lord I pray you give___ me___

Repeat to Fade

HEAVEN

Words and Music by BRYAN ADAMS
and JIM VALLANCE

168

HIGHER LOVE

Words and Music by WILL JENNINGS
and STEVE WINWOOD

HOLD ME NOW

Words and Music by TOM BAILEY,
ALANNAH CURRIE and JOE LEEWAY

HOLD ON LOOSELY

Words and Music by DON BARNES,
JEFF CARLISI and JAMES MICHAEL PETERIK

HOT HOT HOT

Words and Music by
ALPHONSUS CASSELL

Moderate Latin Dance

O - lé, o - lé, o - lé, o - lé. O - lé, o - lé, o -

lé, o - lé.

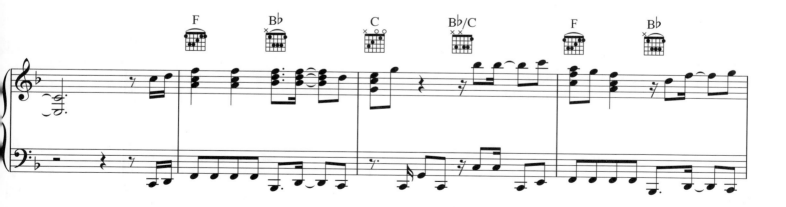

HURTS SO GOOD

Words and Music by JOHN MELLENCAMP
and GEORGE GREEN

I GUESS THAT'S WHY THEY CALL IT THE BLUES

Words and Music by ELTON JOHN,
BERNIE TAUPIN and DAVEY JOHNSTONE

Moderately slow; with a beat

Don't wish it a - way, don't look at it like it's for -
Just stare in - to space; pic - ture my face in your

Instrumental solo

ev - er. Be - tween you ___ and
hands. ___ Live for ___ each

I JUST CALLED TO SAY I LOVE YOU

Words and Music by
STEVIE WONDER

Additional Lyrics

3. No summer's high; no warm July;
   No harvest moon to light one tender August night.
   No autumn breeze; no falling leaves;
   Not even time for birds to fly to southern skies.

4. No Libra sun; no Halloween;
   No giving thanks to all the Christmas joy you bring.
   But what it is, though old so new
   To fill your heart like no three words could ever do.
   Chorus

I LOVE A RAINY NIGHT

Words and Music by EDDIE RABBITT,
EVEN STEVENS and DAVID MALLOY

Well, I love ___ a rain-y night, I love a rain-y night, I love to hear the thun-der, watch the light-ning when it lights up the sky. ___ You know it makes ___ me feel ___ good. Well, I love ___

Omit L.H. on repeat

IT'S MY LIFE

Words and Music by MARK DAVID HOLLIS
and TIM FRIESE-GREENE

*Recorded a half step lower.

JESSIE'S GIRL

Words and Music by
RICK SPRINGFIELD

to be?

Tell me where can I find a _____

wom-an like that?

You know I wish that I had Jes-sie's girl. _____ I wish that I had

Jes-sie's girl. _____ I want Jes-sie's girl. _____

Where can I find a _____ wom-an like that? Like

rit.

JUMP

Words and Music by DAVID LEE ROTH, EDWARD VAN HALEN,
ALEX VAN HALEN and MICHAEL ANTHONY

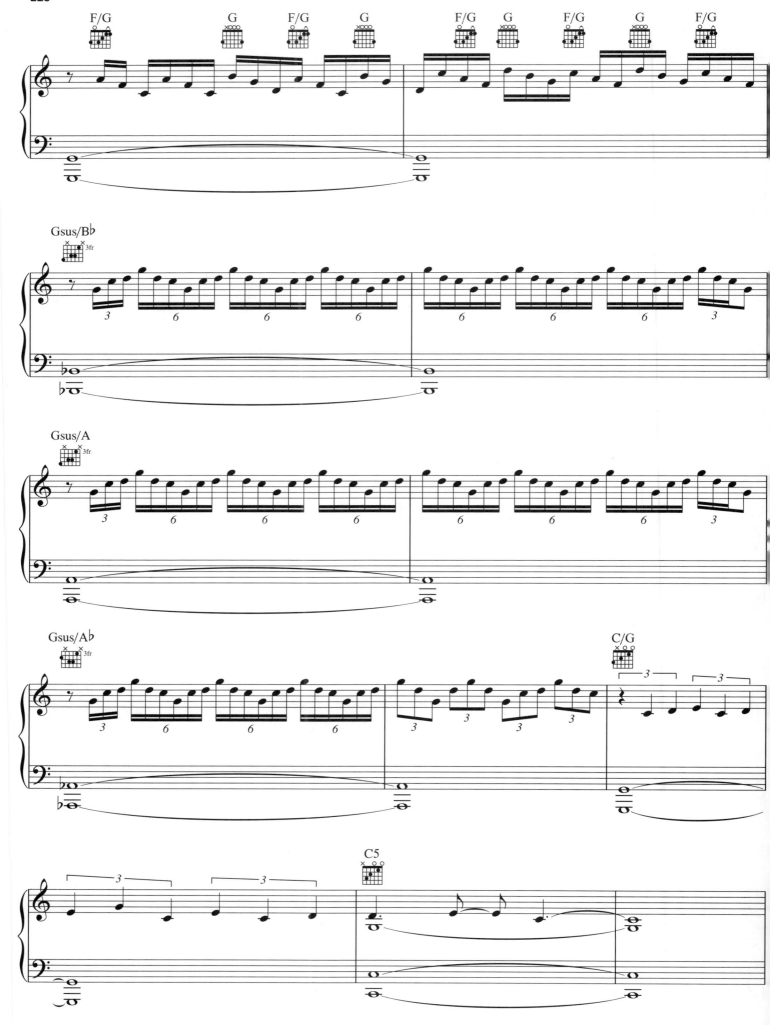

KISS ON MY LIST

Words and Music by JANNA ALLEN
and DARYL HALL

D.S. and Fade

Be - cause your

LADY

Words and Music by
NICHOLAS CALDWELL

Recorded a half-step higher.

You say you love me, la-dy. _____ Girl, I hope you do.

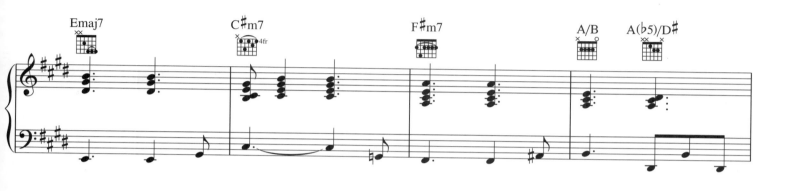

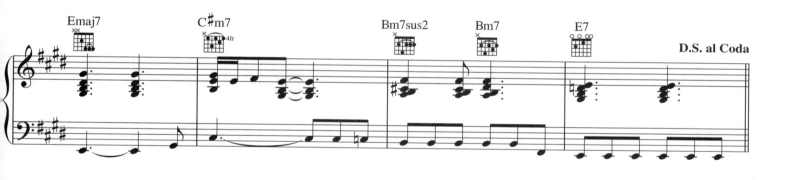

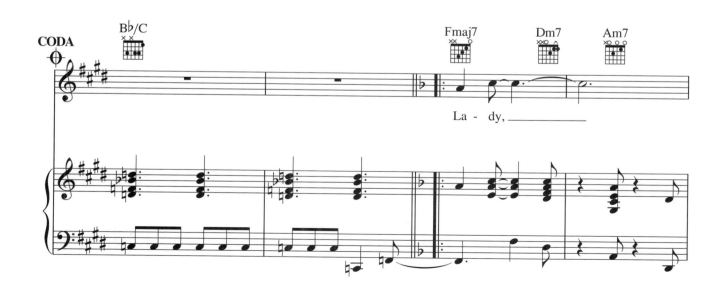

La - dy, _____

real-ly, real-ly love you, girl. ___ La - dy, ___ and no pow - er, no pow - er,

ba - by, can keep us a - part. You're en - graved ___ in my

heart. ___ Do you hear me pret-ty la - dy? ___

Repeat, vocal ad lib. and Fade | **Optional Ending**

MISSING YOU

Words and Music by JOHN WAITE,
CHARLES SANFORD and MARK LEONARD

LADY IN RED

Words and Music by
CHRIS DeBURGH

LEGS

Words and Music by BILLY F GIBBONS,
DUSTY HILL and FRANK BEARD

won - derin' how to feel them. Would you get be-
she knows what to do.
all of the time.

Ev - 'ry - bod - y
Stays out at

(8vb)

C#5

hind them if you could on - ly find them?
wants to see, see if she can use it.
night, mov - in' through time.

A5

She's my ba - by, she's my ba-
She's so fine. She's all
Whoa, I want her. Shit, I got to

8vb

loco

MAN IN THE MIRROR

Words and Music by
GLEN BALLARD and SIEDAH GARRETT

MANIC MONDAY

Words and Music by PRINCE

MATERIAL GIRL

Words and Music by PETER BROWN
and ROBERT RANS

NASTY

Words and Music by JAMES HARRIS III,
TERRY LEWIS and JANET JACKSON

this. Lis - ten up. *Sung:* I'm not a prude. __ I

just want some re - spect. __ So close the door __ if you want me to __ re - spond. __

'Cause pri - va - cy __ is my mid - dle name, my

last name is con - trol. __ *Spoken:* No, my first name ain't Ba - by, it's

Jan - et, Miss Jack - son if you're nas - ty. *Sung:* Nas - ty, nas - ty boys —

don't mean a thing. — Oh, you nas - ty boys.

Nas - ty, nas - ty boys, — don't ev - er change. —

Oh, you nas - ty boys. Nas - ty boys, don't mean a thing. —

Who's that in that nas - ty car? __ (Nas - ty boys.) __

Who's that eat - in' that nas - ty food? __ (Nas - ty boys.) __

Who's jam-min' to my nas - ty groove? __ (Nas - ty boys.) __ La - dies? *Sung:* Nas - ty ____ boys

don't mean a thing. __ Oh, you nas - ty boys.

NOTHING'S GONNA STOP US NOW

Words and Music by DIANE WARREN
and ALBERT HAMMOND

Moderate Rock

Look - ing in your eyes, I see ___ a par - a - dise, this world ___ that I found ___ is too good ___ to be true. ___ Stand - ing here be - side you, want ___

___ so glad I found you, I'm ___ not gon - na lose you, what - ev - er it takes ___ I will stay ___ here with you. ___ Take ___ you to the good times, see ___

OH SHERRIE

Words and Music by STEVE PERRY, RANDY GOODRUM,
BILL CUOMO and CRAIG KRAMPF

You've should -'ve been

ON THE WINGS OF LOVE

Words and Music by JEFFREY OSBORNE
and PETER SCHLESS

Just smile ___ for me ___ and let ___ the day ___ be - gin. ___
You look ___ at me ___ and I ___ be - gin ___ to melt ___

You are ___ the sun - shine ___ that lights my heart ___ with - in. ___
just like ___ the snow when ___ a ray of sun ___ is felt. ___

THE SEARCH IS OVER

Words and Music by JAMES M. PETERIK
and FRANK SULLIVAN

SEVEN BRIDGES ROAD

Words and Music by
STEPHEN T. YOUNG

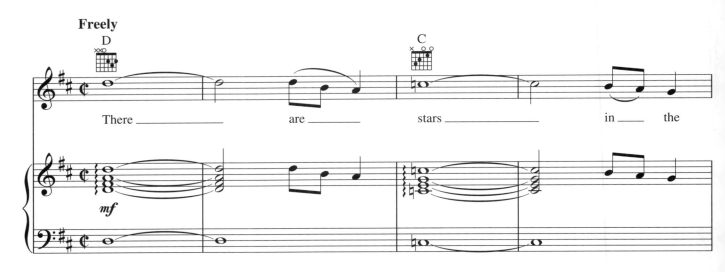

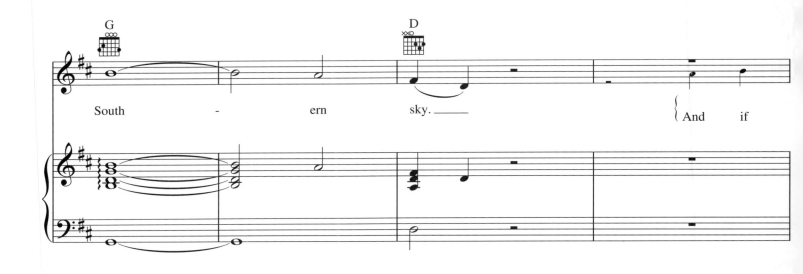

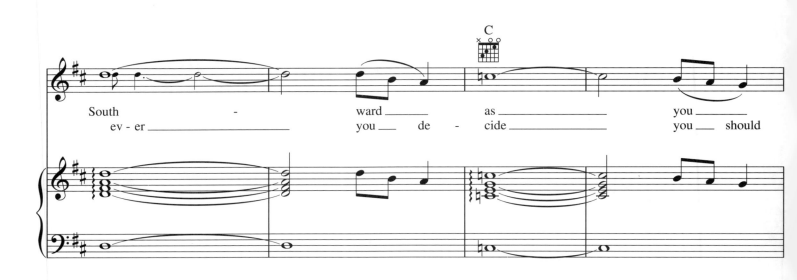

Bright Country

SHOULD I STAY OR SHOULD I GO

Words and Music by
MICK JONES and JOE STRUMMER

SISTER CHRISTIAN

Words and Music by
KELLY KEAGY

SOMEWHERE OUT THERE

from AN AMERICAN TAIL

Words and Music by JAMES HORNER,
BARRY MANN and CYNTHIA WEIL

Moderately, with expression

D.S. al Coda

STEPPIN' OUT

Words and Music by
JOE JACKSON

Recorded a half step higher.

Cm7
3fr
D♭
E♭
3fr
that shine.
E - lec - tric - i -
be - hind.
Don't you won - der
Cm7
3fr
D♭
D♭/E♭
ty so fine;
look and dry your eyes.
what we'll find,
step - pin' out to - night?
Fmaj9
E♭maj7/F
Dm7/F
A♭/F
B♭/F
E♭/F
B♭/F

Eb
Cm7
Db
get in - to a car and drive
We'll be there in just a while,
Db/Eb
Fmaj9
to the oth - er side.
if you fol - low me.
Me, babe, step - pin'
Ebmaj7/F
Dm7/F
Ab/F
Bb/F
Eb/F
out, in - to the
Bb/F
Db/F
Eb/F
Ab/F
Eb/F
night, in - to the light.

STRAIGHT UP

Words and Music by ELLIOT WOLFF

STRAY CAT STRUT

Words and Music by
BRIAN SETZER

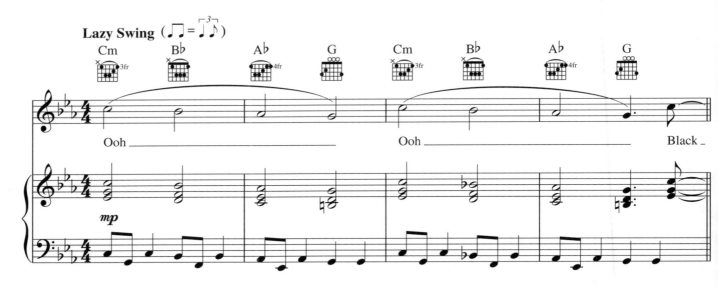

Ooh _____ Ooh _____ Black _

_____ and orange stray cat sit-tin' on a fence. Ain't _

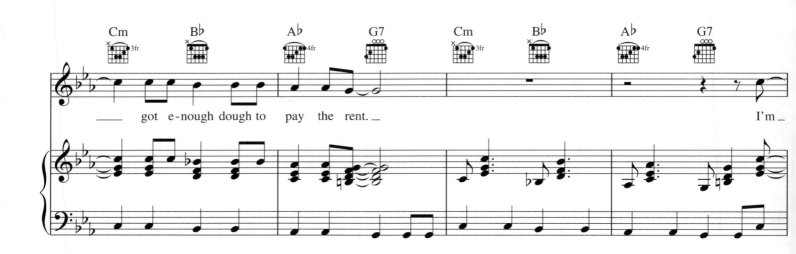

_____ got e-nough dough to pay the rent. _ I'm _

TAKE MY BREATH AWAY
(Love Theme)
from the Paramount Picture TOP GUN

Words and Music by GIORGIO MORODER
and TOM WHITLOCK

Watch-ing ev-'ry mo-tion in ___ my fool-ish lov-er's game; ___ on this end-less o-cean, fi-
Watch-ing, I keep wait-ing, still ___ an-tic-i-pat-ing love, ___ nev-er hes-i-tat-ing to ___
Watch-ing ev-'ry mo-tion in ___ this fool-ish lov-er's game; ___ haunt-ed by the no-tion some-

WHAT'S LOVE GOT TO DO WITH IT

Words and Music by
TERRY BRITTEN and GRAHAM LYLE

Slow Rock

TEMPTED

Words and Music by CHRISTOPHER DIFFORD
and GLENN TILBROOK

* Recorded a half step lower.

TIME AFTER TIME

Words and Music by CYNDI LAUPER
and ROB HYMAN

UP WHERE WE BELONG

from the Paramount Picture AN OFFICER AND A GENTLEMAN

Words by WILL JENNINGS
Music by BUFFY SAINTE-MARIE and JACK NITZSCHE

VIDEO KILLED THE RADIO STAR

Words and Music by BRUCE WOOLLEY,
TREVOR HORN and GEOFF DOWNES

Bright tempo

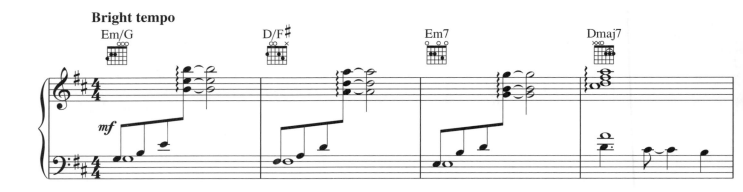

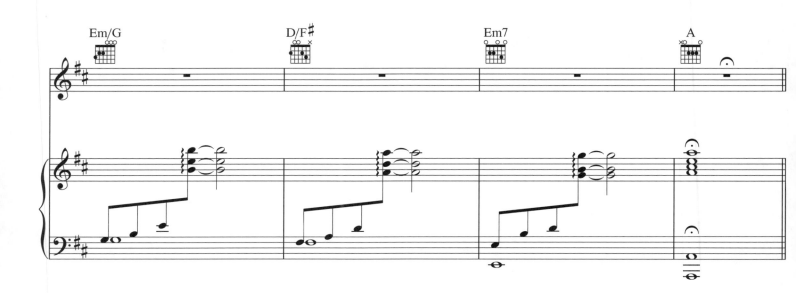

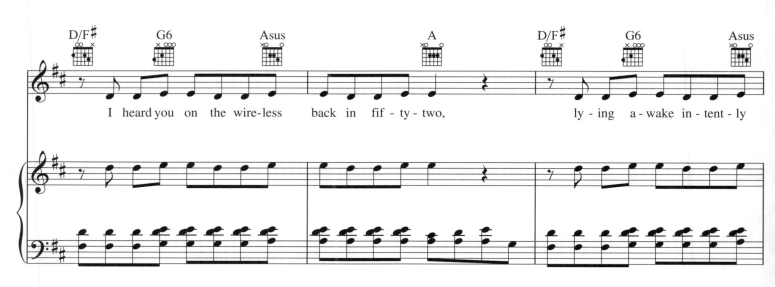

I heard you on the wire-less back in fif-ty-two, ly-ing a-wake in-tent-ly

WANTED DEAD OR ALIVE

Words and Music by
JON BON JOVI and RICHIE SAMBORA

Moderately slow

It's

Dm   D   Dsus4   D   C(add D)   G

1. all the same,___ on - ly the names___ will change,_____
2. times I sleep,___ some - times it's not___ for days,_____ and
3. *Instrumental* _____

THE WARRIOR

Words and Music by NICK GILDER
and HOLLY KNIGHT

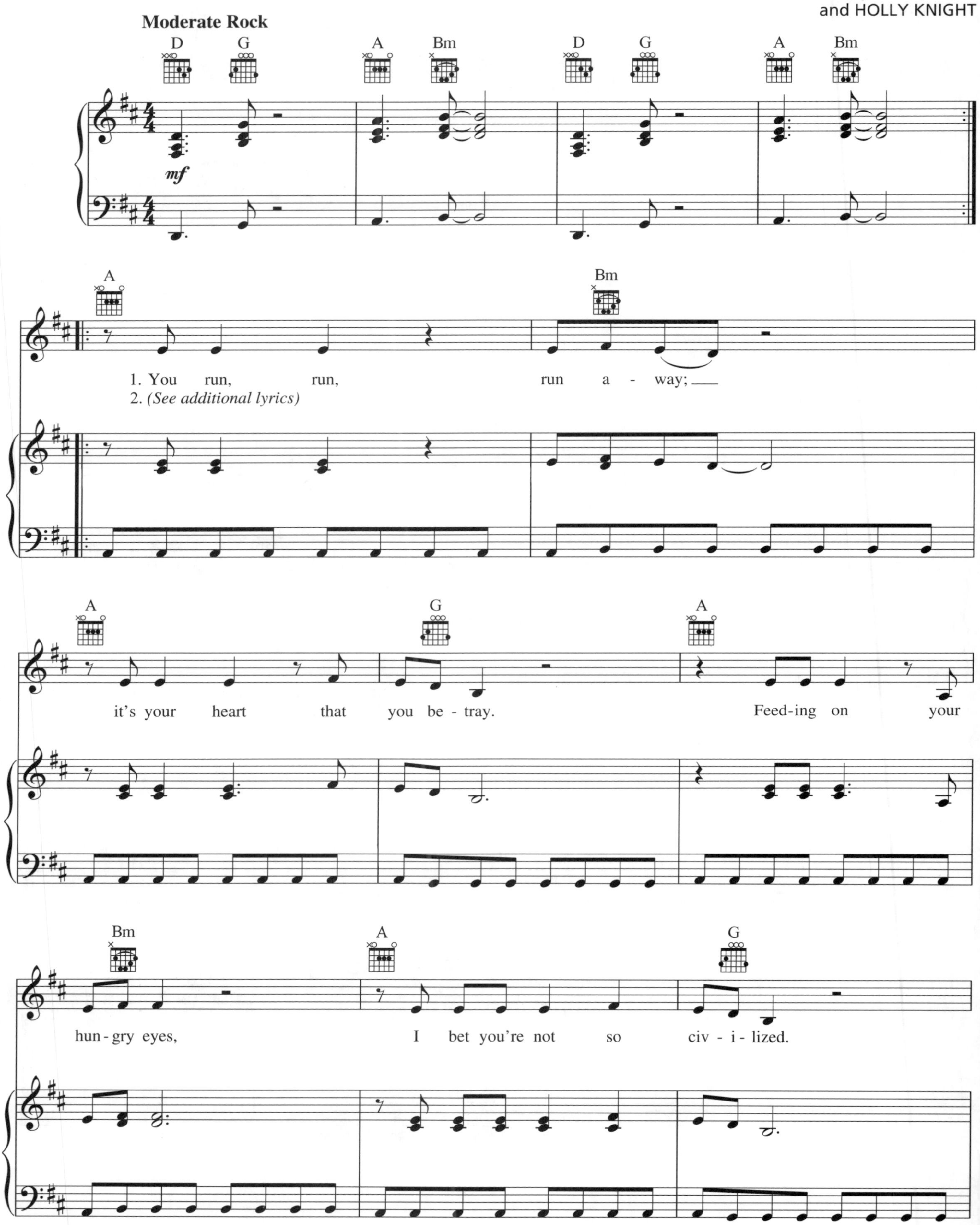

Moderate Rock
D G A Bm D G A Bm
mf
A Bm
1. You run, run, run a - way;
2. (See additional lyrics)
A G A
it's your heart that you be - tray. Feed-ing on your
Bm A G
hun-gry eyes, I bet you're not so civ - i - lized.

the war - ri - or

the war - ri - or.

D.S. and Fade

Additional Lyrics

2. You talk, talk, you talk to me,
   Your eyes touch me physically.
   Stay with me, we'll take the night
   As passion takes another bite.
   Who's the hunter, who's the game?
   I feel the beat, call your name.
   I hold you close in victory.
   I don't wanna tame your animal style;
   You won't be caged in the call of the wild.
   Chorus

WE ARE THE WORLD

Words and Music by LIONEL RICHIE
and MICHAEL JACKSON

WHAT ABOUT LOVE?

Words and Music by BRIAN ALLEN,
SHERON ALTON and JIM VALLANCE

WHITE WEDDING

Words and Music by
BILLY IDOL

Fast Rock

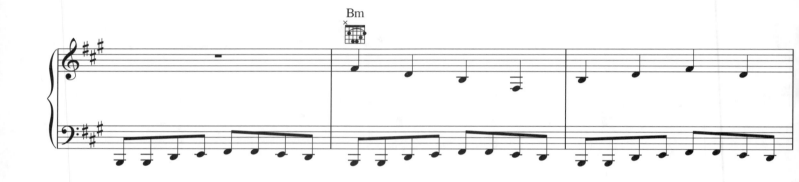

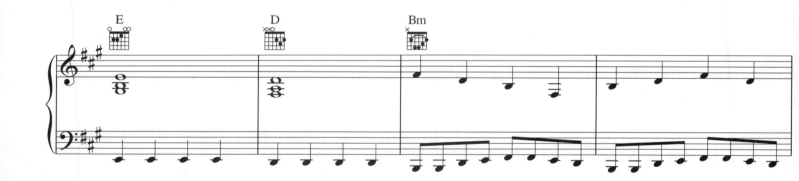

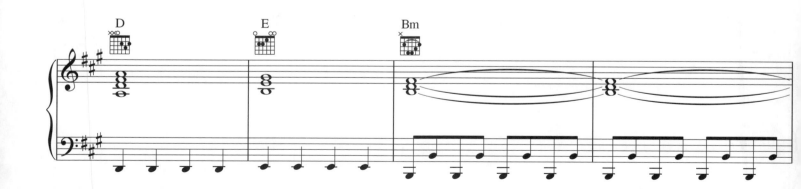

HAL•LEONARD ESSENTIAL SONGS

Play the best songs from the Roaring '20s to today! Each collection features up to 100 of the most memorable songs of each decade, arranged in Piano/Vocal/Guitar format or in our world-famous, patented E-Z Play® Today notation. Each book also includes info about the composers or from the Billboard charts: the songs' peak position and the year they charted.

ESSENTIAL SONGS – THE 1920s

Over 100 songs that shaped the decade, including: Ain't We Got Fun? • All by Myself • April Showers • Basin Street Blues • Bill • The Birth of the Blues • Blue Skies • Bye Bye Blackbird • California, Here I Come • Can't Help Lovin' Dat Man • Chicago (That Toddlin' Town) • Five Foot Two, Eyes of Blue (Has Anybody Seen My Girl?) • I Can't Give You Anything but Love • I Wanna Be Loved by You • I'm Looking Over a Four Leaf Clover • If You Knew Susie (Like I Know Susie) • Indian Love Call • Let a Smile Be Your Umbrella • Look for the Silver Lining • Makin' Whoopee! • Manhattan • Moonlight and Roses (Bring Mem'ries of You) • My Blue Heaven • Ol' Man River • Puttin' On the Ritz • St. Louis Blues • Second Hand Rose • Stardust • Thou Swell • Toot, Toot, Tootsie! (Good-bye!) • 'Way down Yonder in New Orleans • Who's Sorry Now • Yes Sir, That's My Baby • and more.
00311200 Piano/Vocal/Guitar......................$24.95
00100214 E-Z Play Today #23 ....$19.94

ESSENTIAL SONGS – THE 1930s

Over 100 essential songs from the 1930s, including: All the Things You Are • April in Paris • Autumn in New York • Body and Soul • Cheek to Cheek • Cherokee (Indian Love Song) • Easy to Love (You'd Be So Easy to Love) • Falling in Love with Love • Georgia on My Mind • Heart and Soul • How Deep Is the Ocean (How High Is the Sky) • I'll Be Seeing You • I've Got My Love to Keep Me Warm • In a Sentimental Mood • In the Mood • Isn't It Romantic? • The Lady Is a Tramp • Mood Indigo • My Funny Valentine • Pennies from Heaven • September Song • You Are My Sunshine • and more.
00311193 Piano/Vocal/Guitar $24.95
00100206 E-Z Play Today #24 ....$19.95

ESSENTIAL SONGS – THE 1940s

An amazing collection of over 100 songs that came out of the 1940s, including: Ac-cent-tchu-ate the Positive • Anniversary Song • Be Careful, It's My Heart • Bewitched • Boogie Woogie Bugle Boy • Don't Get Around Much Anymore • Have I Told You Lately That I Love You • I'll Remember April • Is You Is, or Is You Ain't (Ma' Baby) • It Could Happen to You • It Might As Well Be Spring • Route 66 • Sentimental Journey • Stella by Starlight • The Surrey with the Fringe on Top • Take the "A" Train • They Say It's Wonderful • This Nearly Was Mine • You'd Be So Nice to Come Home To • You're Nobody 'til Somebody Loves You • and more.
00311192 P/V/G $24.95
00100207 E-Z Play Today #25 ....$19.95

ESSENTIAL SONGS – THE 1950s

Over 100 pivotal songs from the 1950s, including: All Shook Up • At the Hop • Blueberry Hill • Bye Bye Love • Chantilly Lace • Don't Be Cruel (To a Heart That's True) • Fever • Great Balls of Fire • High Hopes • Kansas City • Love and Marriage • Mister Sandman • Mona Lisa • (You've Got) Personality • Rock Around the Clock • Sea of Love • Sixteen Tons • Smoke Gets in Your Eyes • Tennessee Waltz • Tom Dooley • Twilight Time • Wear My Ring Around Your Neck • Wonderful! Wonderful! • and more.
00311191 Piano/Vocal/Guitar $24.95
00100208 E-Z Play Today #51 ....$19.95

ESSENTIAL SONGS – THE 1960s

Over 100 '60s essentials, including: Baby Love • Barbara Ann • Born to Be Wild • California Girls • Can't Buy Me Love • Dancing in the Street • Downtown • Good Vibrations • Hang on Sloopy • Hey Jude • I Heard It Through the Grapevine • It's Not Unusual • My Guy • Respect • Something • Spooky • Stand by Me • Stop! in the Name of Love • Suspicious Minds • A Time for Us (Love Theme) • Twist and Shout • Will You Love Me Tomorrow (Will You Still Love Me Tomorrow) • Yesterday • You Keep Me Hangin' On • and more.
00311190 Piano/Vocal/Guitar $24.95
00100209 E-Z Play Today #52 ....$19.95

ESSENTIAL SONGS – THE 1970s

A fantastic collection of over 80 of the best songs from the '70s, including: ABC • Afternoon Delight • American Pie • American Woman • At Seventeen • Baker Street • Band on the Run • Bohemian Rhapsody • The Boys Are Back in Town • Come Sail Away • Da Ya Think I'm Sexy • Do You Know Where You're Going To? • Dust in the Wind • Feelings (¿Dime?) • Hot Child in the City • I Feel the Earth Move • I'll Be There • Knock Three Times • Let It Be • Morning Has Broken • Smoke on the Water • Take a Chance on Me • The Way We Were • What's Going On • You Are the Sunshine of My Life • You Light Up My Life • You're So Vain • Your Song • and more.
00311189 Piano/Vocal/Guitar $24.95
00100210 E-Z Play Today #53 ....$19.95

ESSENTIAL SONGS – THE 1980s

Over 70 classics from the age of new wave, power pop, and hair metal, including: Abracadabra • Against All Odds (Take a Look at Me Now) • Axel F • Call Me • Centerfold • Could I Have This Dance • Didn't We Almost Have It All • Don't You (Forget About Me) • Ebony and Ivory • Footloose • The Heat Is On • Higher Love • Hurts So Good • Jump • Love Shack • Man in the Mirror • Manic Monday • Material Girl • Rosanna • The Safety Dance • Sister Christian • Somewhere Out There • Take My Breath Away (Love Theme) • Time After Time • Up Where We Belong • We Are the World • What's Love Got to Do with It • and more.
00311188 Piano/Vocal/Guitar $24.95
00100210 E-Z Play Today #54..............$19.95

ESSENTIAL SONGS – THE 1990s

68 essential songs from the 1990s featuring country crossover, swing revival, the birth of grunge, and much more. Songs include: All 4 Love • Blaze of Glory • Blue • Can You Feel the Love Tonight • Change the World • Come to My Window • (Everything I Do) I Do It for You • Fields of Gold • From a Distance • I Finally Found Someone • I Will Remember You • Ironic • Janie's Got a Gun • Livin' La Vida Loca • More Than Words • Semi-Charmed Life • Smells like Teen Spirit • This Kiss • Two Princes • Under the Bridge • Walking in Memphis • Zoot Suit Riot • and more.
00311187 Piano/Vocal/Guitar $24.95

ESSENTIAL SONGS – THE 2000s

58 of the best songs that brought in the new millennium, including: Accidentally in Love • Always • Beautiful • Breathe • Calling All Angels • Clocks • Complicated • Don't Know Why • Get the Party Started • Give Me Just One Night (Una Noche) • Hey Ya! • I Hope You Dance • Jenny from the Block • 1985 • Out of My Head (Into Your Head) • She Bangs • So Yesterday • Somewhere Out There • The Space Between • Thank You • There You'll Be • This Love • A Thousand Miles • Underneath Your Clothes • Wherever You Will Go • Who Let the Dogs Out • You Raise Me Up • and more.
00311186 Piano/Vocal/Guitar ....$24.